PRO SPORTS
BIOGRAPHIES

J. J. WATT

by Elizabeth Raum

AMICUS HIGH INTEREST • AMICUS INK

Amicus High Interest and Amicus Ink are imprints of Amicus
P.O. Box 1329, Mankato, MN 56002
www.amicuspublishing.us

Library of Congress Cataloging-in-Publication Data
Names: Raum, Elizabeth, author.
Title: J.J. Watt / by Elizabeth Raum.
Description: Mankato, Minnesota : Amicus, 2018. | Series: Amicus High Interest. Pro Sports Biographies | Includes index. | Audience: K to Grade 3.
Identifiers: LCCN 2016058342 (print) | LCCN 2017005824 (ebook) | ISBN 9781681511368 (library binding) | ISBN 9781681521671 (pbk.) | ISBN 9781681512266 (ebook)
Subjects: LCSH: Watt, J. J., 1989---Juvenile literature. | Football players--United States--Biography--Juvenile literature.
Classification: LCC GV939.W362 R38 2018 (print) | LCC GV939.W362 (ebook) | DDC 796.332092 [B] --dc23
LC record available at https://lccn.loc.gov/2016058342

Photo Credits: Bill Baptist via AP cover; Ronald C. Modra/Sports Imagery/Getty Images 2; AP Photo/David J. Phillip 4–5, 12–13; John Rowland/Southcreek Global/ZUMAPRESS 7, 8; AP Photo/Houston Chronicle, Brett Coomer 11; Al Pereira/Getty Images 15; Darren Walsh/Chelsea FC via Getty Images 16–17; Trask Smith/ZUMA Wire/Alamy Live News 18–19; Bob Levey/Getty Images Sport 20–21; AP Photo/Scott Boehm 22

Editor: Wendy Dieker
Designer: Aubrey Harper
Photo Researcher: Holly Young

Printed in the United States of America

HC 10 9 8 7 6 5 4 3 2 1
PB 10 9 8 7 6 5 4 3 2 1

TABLE OF CONTENTS

4

WATCH OUT!

Here comes number 99. It's J. J. Watt! He's a **defensive end** with the Houston Texans. He tackles. He swats the ball down. Watt is one of the best at stopping the football.

J. J. Watt's full name is Justin James Watt.

BECOMING A BADGER

Watt grew up in Wisconsin. He dreamed of playing football at the University of Wisconsin. He was not good enough. He practiced hard. In 2008, he finally got in.

The badger is the University of Wisconsin's mascot.

HARD WORK

Watt kept practicing. He worked hard to be the best defensive end. He watched videos of games to study the best moves. By 2010, he was a college football star.

A STAR

In 2011, Watt turned **pro**. He joined the Houston Texans. The next year, he made the **Pro Bowl** team. Only the best players make the Pro Bowl team.

Watt was the Pro Bowl team captain in 2014.

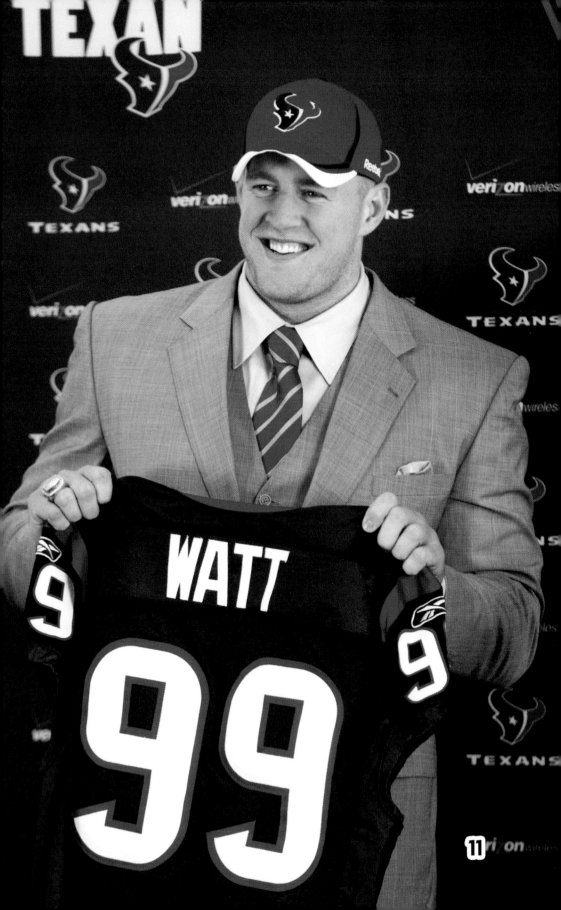

SACKS

Watt tackles the **quarterback**. That's called a **sack**. He made more than 20 sacks in one season. Then he did it again. He's the first **NFL** player to get 20 sacks in two different seasons.

NUMBER ONE

Every year, NFL players vote on the top 100 players. Watt has been on the list several times. In 2015, players voted him the best football player in the NFL.

The Associated Press named Watt "Defensive Player of the Year" three times.

STAYING FIT

Watt trains hard. He works out every day. He runs. He lifts weights. Watt sleeps 10 hours a night. He eats healthy meals. Watt works hard to keep his body fit.

HELPING KIDS

Watt got to play sports after school. He knows some kids can't. It costs too much. Watt wants to help those kids. He set up a fund. It helps pay the **fees**.

Watt sometimes visits sick kids in the hospital. They are happy to see him.

LOOKING AHEAD

J. J. Watt loves football. Some day he will stop playing. He wants to move back to Wisconsin. He may coach high school football. He may even coach his old team.

Watt bought a home in the Wisconsin woods. He likes to walk his land. It helps him think.

JUST THE FACTS

Born: March 22, 1989

Hometown: Waukesha, Wisconsin

College: University of Wisconsin

Joined the pros: 2011

Position: Defensive End

Stats: www.nfl.com/player/j.j.watt/2495488/careerstats

Accomplishments:

- First NFL player to record over 20 sacks in a single season twice

- Named to NFL's Top 100 Players: 2014 (#12), 2015 (#1), 2016 (#3)

- NFL Pro Bowl appearances: 2012, 2013, 2014, 2015

- AP Defensive Player of the Year: 2012, 2014, 2015

WORDS TO KNOW

defensive end – a football player who attacks the quarterback or stops players running with the ball

fee – money charged to do something

NFL (National Football League) – the organization that makes the rules for the professional American football league

pro – short for professional; a person who is paid to play sports

Pro Bowl – a football game played by the best football players from different NFL teams

quarterback – the leader of the offense, or the team trying to score points; this player often passes the ball to others to try to score

sack – to tackle the quarterback

LEARN MORE

Books

Adamson, Thomas K. *The Houston Texans Story*. Minneapolis: Bellwether Media, 2017.

Scheff, Matt. *J. J. Watt*. Minneapolis: Abdo Publishing Co., 2016.

Websites

J. J. Watt | ESPN
www.espn.com/nfl/player/stats/_/id/13979/jj-watt

Justin J. Watt Foundation
http://jjwfoundation.org/

Official Site of the Houston Texans
www.houstontexans.com

INDEX

Every effort has been made to ensure that these websites are appropriate for children. However, because of the nature of the Internet, it is impossible to guarantee that these sites will remain active indefinitely or that their contents will not be altered.